Getting To Know...

Nature's Children

MUSKRATS

Laima Dingwall

PUBLISHER	Joseph R. DeVarennes
PUBLICATION DIRECTOR	Kenneth H. Pearson
MANAGING EDITOR	Valerie Wyatt
SERIES ADVISOR	Merebeth Switzer
SERIES CONSULTANT	Michael Singleton
CONSULTANTS	Ross James Kay McKeever Dr. Audrey N. Tomera
ADVISORS	Roger Aubin Robert Furlonger Gaston Lavoie
EDITORIAL SUPERVISOR	Jocelyn Smyth
PRODUCTION MANAGER	Don Markle
PRODUCTION ASSISTANTS	Penelope Moir Steve Soloman
EDITORS	Mary Frances Coady Katherine Farris Cristel Kleitsch Elizabeth MacLeod Anne Minguet-Patocka Sarah Reid Cathy Ripley Eleanor Tourtel Kathy Vanderlinden Karin Velcheff
PHOTO EDITORS	Laurel Haslett Pamela Martin
DESIGN	Annette Tatchell
CARTOGRAPHER	Jane Davie
PUBLICATION ADMINISTRATION	Kathy Kishimoto Monique Lemonnier
ARTISTS	Marianne Collins Pat Ivy Greg Ruhl Mary Theberge

This series is approved and recommended by the Federation of Ontario Naturalists.

Canadian Cataloguing in Publication Data

Dingwall, Laima, 1953-
Muskrats

(Getting to know—nature's children)
Includes index.
ISBN 0-7172-1921-6

1. Muskrats—Juvenile literature.
I. Title. II. Series.

QL737.R638D56 1985 j599.3233 C85-098725-3

Printed and Bound in Canada

Have you ever wondered . . .

What small, furry North American animal is a good swimmer and builds a lodge home in the water? If you answered a beaver, you are right. But there is another animal that does this too. Here is another clue: in summer, this animal also builds floating dining rooms and in winter, special ice huts.

If you guessed muskrat this time, you are right! Read on to find out more about this busy builder. But first let's take a look at a muskrat baby . . .

Meet a Baby Muskrat

By the time it pokes its shiny little nose out of the nursery den for the first time, a baby muskrat, or kit, is already able to swim. It follows its brothers and sisters into the water and paddles furiously out into the marsh.

Not far away its mother munches on some cattails. The evening air is filled with frog song, and the water glows red in the setting sun. A busy life of building and diving and swimming is about to begin for this young muskrat.

Muskrat kits have much darker and woollier coats than full-grown muskrats.

Family Ties

It is not surprising that people often get the beaver and the muskrat mixed up. After all, both animals are built for life in the water. But the muskrat is not even part of the beaver family. It is related to the deer mouse, the harvest mouse, the woodrat, the lemming, the cotton rat and the vole.

It is easy to tell the muskrat from these rodent relatives. Quite simply, it is larger than any other mouse or rat found in North America. From the tip of its quivering little nose to the end of its long, skinny tail, the muskrat measures about 50 centimetres (20 inches), but half of that length is tail. The muskrat is also almost 50 times heavier than the average mouse, weighing in at about one kilogram (2 pounds).

You'll be excused for not noticing the muskrat's tiny ears. They are almost hidden in long fur.

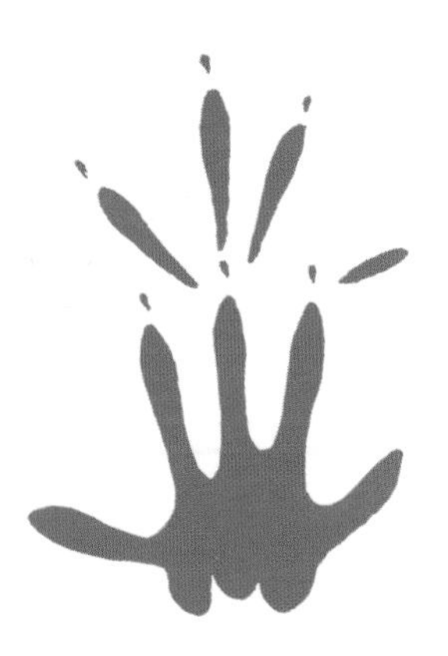

Muskrat tracks

A Muskrat by Any Other Name

The muskrat goes by many names. The Algonquin Indians called it *musquash* while the Huron Indians called it *ondatra*. It has even been called mud cat and mud beaver.

How did it get the name muskrat? It makes a powerful, sweet-smelling liquid called *musk* in two glands under its tail. The muskrat uses this musk at mating time and to mark its territory. And it looks very much like a plump *rat* that grew glossy, rich fur. Put the two words together and what do you get? Right . . . musk-rat!

From Coast to Coast

Muskrats are found from Alaska and northern Canada to the Gulf of Mexico in the south and from the Atlantic Ocean right across to the Pacific. In fact, muskrats are spread over a greater area of North America than almost any other mammal.

Where muskrats live in North America.

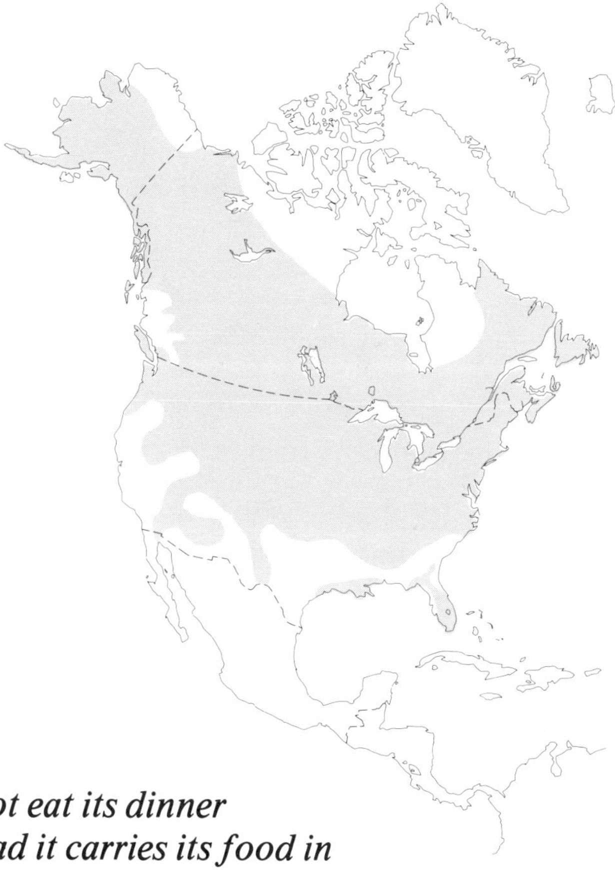

A muskrat does not eat its dinner underwater. Instead it carries its food in its front teeth to the surface and dines on a floating feeding station.

Choosing a Home

The muskrat is fussy about where it makes its home. It looks for three things. Can you guess what is at the top of its list? If you said water, congratulations. A freshwater marsh or a quiet pond, a slow-moving stream or river or lake are good places for a muskrat home.

But if the water is too deep—deeper than the deep end of a swimming pool—there probably will not be any tasty plants growing on the bottom. No food, no muskrat! And if the marsh is too shallow—shallower than a bathtub—the pond will probably freeze right through in winter making it impossible for the muskrat to live there. And so the second thing on a muskrat's list is water that is just the right depth. Finally, the muskrat looks for lots of plants, especially cattails and bulrushes growing near the shore. It not only eats the plants, it uses them to build with too.

The muskrat's tiny hand-like front paws are useful for grabbing and holding food underwater and on the shore.

Many Muskrats

As many as 32 muskrats may share a pond the size of a football field, if there is enough food available. But if the food supply is low, only a few muskrats will live in the same pond.

Wherever the muskrat lives it stakes out a home territory. To do this it sprays its musk scent on trees and other landmarks. These musk messages tell other muskrats: "This territory is already taken. Stay out." Intruders who ignore the warning are met with bared teeth and a snarl.

Imagine this muskrat's surprise when it looked down and saw its own reflection!

Front paw

Rear paw

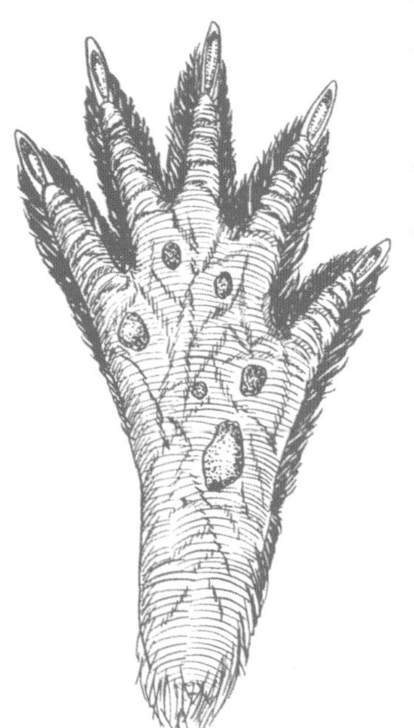

Super Swimmer

It would take an Olympic swimmer to beat a muskrat in a race because a muskrat can swim up to five kilometres (2-3 miles) an hour. How can such a small animal swim so fast?

First the muskrat streamlines its body by folding its front paws close to its chest. That way it can effortlessly cut through the water, like a torpedo. Then it turns on the paddle power. The muskrat has big hind feet that are made even bigger by a fringe of stiff hair around them. These big paddle-like feet help to power the muskrat forward. For extra speed, it swishes its long tail back and forth. The tail also acts like a ship's rudder and helps the muskrat change directions in the water.

Waterproof Fur Coat

The muskrat's glossy waterproof coat also helps make it a good swimmer. How? Air bubbles get trapped in the fur, helping the muskrat stay afloat.

The muskrat's coat is really two coats in one. Underneath the first coat of shiny waterproof guard hairs is an inner coat of short thick fur. The outer hairs keep the muskrat dry all year round. The inner fur holds in body heat to keep it warm in winter.

To avoid being seen, muskrats often swim close to shore among the reeds.

Diving Champ

The muskrat dives underwater to find food or build a lodge. It usually stays for no more than a few minutes at a time—just long enough to bite off a tasty root or plant and swim back up to the surface. But if the muskrat is trying to escape an enemy, it can stay under for more than 12 minutes without coming up for air. How does the muskrat do it? It relaxes its muscles and slows down its heart rate. This way the muskrat's air supply lasts longer. Besides carrying air in its lungs as we all do, the muskrat carries an extra supply in its muscles as well.

The muskrat escapes most of its enemies by diving underwater.

Underwater Worker

If you had to carry things underwater in your mouth, you would end up with a mouthful of water. But not the muskrat. Its four front carrying teeth are in front of its lips instead of behind them like yours are. When it has to carry something underwater it closes its lips to shut out the water, leaving its four front teeth free to do the work.

The muskrat also has a way of keeping water out of its ears and nose. Small skin flaps in its ears and nose close when it dives. They open again at the surface so the muskrat can hear and breathe.

The muskrat's four front teeth are not only chisel sharp, but they're dark yellow too.

Muskrat Munchies

After snoozing most of the day, the muskrat slips quietly into the water at night in search of food. Its favorite munchies are cattails, but it will also eat other plants and weeds that grow in and around its home. And it will even catch frogs or fish and dig mussels and clams out of the bottom mud.

Floating Dining Room

Sometimes muskrats build a private dining room on top of a floating raft of reeds. These feeding stations are made of weeds and plants. They are very private indeed—just big enough for one muskrat. Inside the muskrat can eat in safety, out of sight of hungry predators.

Muskrats that live in warm climates use these floating feeding stations all year round. But muskrats in cold climates build sturdier winter shelters called lodges.

A list of the muskrat's favorite foods would not be complete without cattails, smartweed, white water lily and spatterdock.

Lodge Building

Have you ever seen something that looks like a miniature haystack hidden among the cattails at the edge of a pond? If so, you were probably looking at a muskrat's lodge. Many muskrats build these lodges as a bedroom, a winter retreat and a hideaway from enemies.

Lodge building begins in early fall so that the lodge will be ready in plenty of time for the cold winter weather. Cattails, bulrushes and other pond weeds and plants are the main building materials. To collect them, the muskrat swims through the marsh, cutting plants with its sharp front teeth. Then it cements the newly cut stalks into a mound with mud. The muskrat is a tireless worker. It collects more and more plants until the mound rises about one metre (3 feet) out of the water.

This may look like a mini-haystack to you, but to a muskrat it's home.

Finishing Touches

When the mound is big enough, the muskrat dives underwater and begins chewing out a tunnel leading from the bottom of the pile right up into the middle. There it hollows out a small cozy room.

Two tunnels later, the muskrat's lodge is finished. These extra tunnels provide a speedy getaway route in case an enemy should try to surprise the muskrat at home.

Most muskrat lodges are damaged by rooting predators or by ice smashing into them during spring break-up. But if the lodge is not damaged, it will be used another year.

When this happens, several muskrats may work together to repair and add to the lodge until it is twice as big as ordinary lodges. These "monster mounds" may have three or more rooms inside and be home to several muskrats. But usually a muskrat lives alone in its one-muskrat lodge.

Once a muskrat chews out a tunnel it adds the chewed-out material to the outside of its lodge.

A Bank Home

Not all muskrats build lodges. Sometimes there is not enough building material to make one, or the water currents might be too strong and wash the lodge away. Then the muskrat tunnels into the bank of the river, stream or pond.

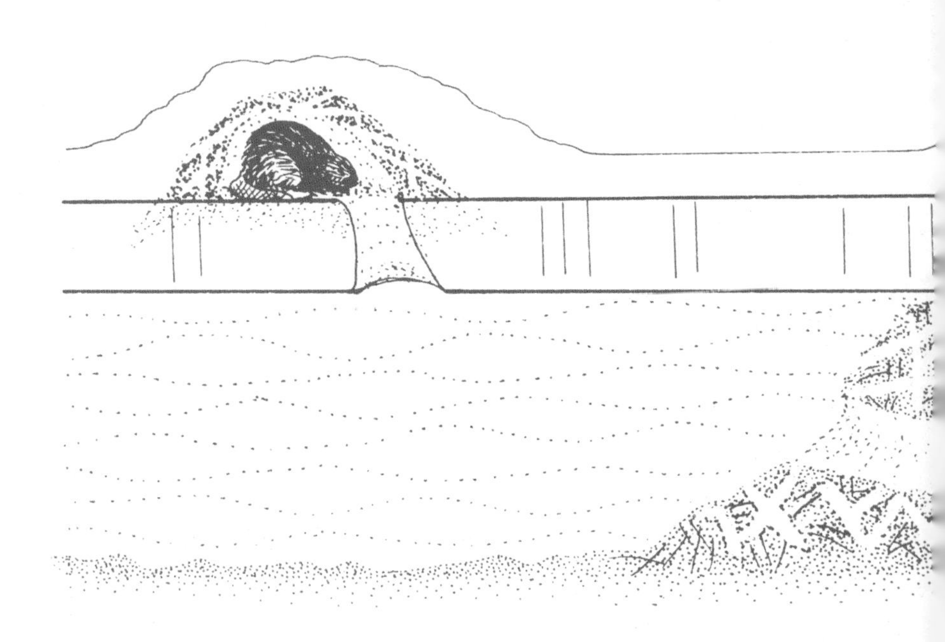

Digging into the bank from underwater, the muskrat carves out a tunnel that slopes upward from the entrance. This way no water will get into its bank home. At the end of the tunnel, it hollows out a small dry room, then digs extra escape routes.

Winter Survival

Muskrats that live in cold-weather climates do not hibernate as some animals do. Instead they are active all winter long—under the ice!

As soon as the pond starts to freeze over, the muskrat swims underwater and chews a hole through the thin, brittle ice. Then it pushes plants and weeds up through this hole.

The muskrat uses them to build a winter feeding station, or "push-up," on top of the ice.

A muskrat may have a string of push-ups going straight out from its lodge. Then if it is swimming underwater it can crawl up into a push-up to eat its dinner or take a rest.

A thick double fur coat keeps the muskrat warm in chilly winter weather.

Life Under the Ice

While other animals pad over the frozen pond in bright sunlight or moonlight, the muskrat moves below the ice in a dimly lit world. Every few days it must check its push-ups to make sure ice has not sealed them closed. And it must search daily for nuts, seeds and berries that fell into the pond before freeze-up. It grubs through the muddy pond bottom, and when it finds something to eat, it carries the food up to a push-up.

By the end of the winter, when food becomes scarce, the muskrat may start to eat away at its lodge or push-ups. After all, these are made of the same plants that the muskrat usually eats. What a bonus for the builder!

The muskrat uses its four front teeth as built-in ice picks to chop holes in the winter ice.

A Smelly Courtship

When a muskrat mates depends on where it lives. Muskrats in warm climates mate all year round, but muskrats in cold climates only mate from spring to early fall.

All mating muskrats have one thing in common—they stink. When a male muskrat is ready to mate, it sprays its powerful smelling musk around its lodge and throughout its territory. This warns other males to stay away and attracts any interested females. Females also leave a musk smell around their homes to tell any nearby males that they are ready to mate.

Male muskrats compete fiercely for a female's attention. They will even fight to win the right to mate with her.

Spring has come and this muskrat will soon be looking for a mate.

Lots of Babies

A month after mating, the female muskrat is ready to give birth. She has anywhere between two and ten babies. She usually nestles her new family into a bank burrow lined with dry grasses. But sometimes she may use a small open nest on the water or borrow an abandoned duck nest for a nursery.

Once her family is born, the female is ready to mate again. In fact, some muskrats may have as many as 20 babies in one year. And, amazing as it may seem, there is a report of one female producing 46 young in one year.

Most muskrat kits are born in snug lodges, some in bank burrows, while others are born in open nests.

Meet the Baby

At birth, a baby muskrat kit is tiny. It barely weighs as much as an egg and is only the length of a crayon. Imagine—you could hold two of these babies in the palm of your hand.

The helpless newborn kit is pink and hairless. Its eyes are closed, and it spends its first few days sleeping and drinking its mother's rich, nourishing milk.

Like most muskrats, this young kit has a lifespan of four years.

Speedy Sprouter

The little creature is not hairless and helpess for long. Within a week, it has grown a thick, coat of sooty colored fur and is crawling around the nursery. At two weeks it has almost doubled its birth size, and its eyes are open. At three weeks the kit is taking short trips out of its nursery into the exciting new world outside.

Soon it stops drinking its mother's milk, and by the time the half-grown kit is six weeks old, it is ready to be out on its own. Off it swims to build a home for itself, usually near its mother's lodge. But some kits seem to find it difficult to leave home so young. These homebodies dig out a tiny room in the side of their mother's lodge or bank burrow and spend their first winter there.

Special Words

Burrow A home that a muskrat digs out of a pond, stream or river bank.

Den Animal home.

Guard hairs Long coarse hairs that make up the outer layer of the muskrat's coat.

Kit A young muskrat.

Lodge A muskrat home built out of plants and mud.

Marsh A flat area of land covered with shallow water.

Mate To come together to produce young.

Musk A powerful smelling liquid produced by the muskrat to mark its territory and attract a mate.

Push-up A winter feeding station for the muskrat.

Territory Area that an animal or group of animals lives in and often defends against animals of the same kind.

INDEX

Cover Photo: Dennis W. Schmidt (Valan Photos)

Photo Credits: Tim Fitzharris (First Light Associated Photographers), pages 4, 16; Norman Lightfoot (Eco-Art Productions), page 7; Wayne Lankinen (Valan Photos), page 8; Bill Ivy, pages 11, 19, 20, 23, 24, 37; Thomas Kitchin (Valan Photos), pages 12, 15, 45; Dennis W. Schmidt (Valan Photos), page 27; Harold V. Green (Valan Photos), page 30; Michel Bourque (Valan Photos), page 33; Brian Milne (Valan Photos), page 37; Robert McCaw (Network Stock Photo File), page 38; V. Claerhout, page 41; Michel Quintin (Valan Photos), page 42.

Getting To Know...

Nature's Children

SALMON

Elma Schemenauer

PUBLISHER	Joseph R. DeVarennes
PUBLICATION DIRECTOR	Kenneth H. Pearson
MANAGING EDITOR	Valerie Wyatt
SERIES ADVISOR	Merebeth Switzer
SERIES CONSULTANT	Michael Singleton
CONSULTANTS	Ross James Kay McKeever Dr. Audrey N. Tomera
ADVISORS	Roger Aubin Robert Furlonger Gaston Lavoie
EDITORIAL SUPERVISOR	Jocelyn Smyth
PRODUCTION MANAGER	Don Markle
PRODUCTION ASSISTANTS	Penelope Moir Steve Soloman
EDITORS	Mary Frances Coady Katherine Farris Cristel Kleitsch Elizabeth MacLeod Anne Minguet-Patocka Sarah Reid Cathy Ripley Eleanor Tourtel Kathy Vanderlinden Karin Velcheff
PHOTO EDITORS	Laurel Haslett Pamela Martin
DESIGN	Annette Tatchell
CARTOGRAPHER	Jane Davie
PUBLICATION ADMINISTRATION	Kathy Kishimoto Monique Lemonnier
ARTISTS	Marianne Collins Pat Ivy Greg Ruhl Mary Theberge

This series is approved and recommended by the Federation of Ontario Naturalists.

Canadian Cataloguing in Publication Data

Schemenauer, Elma.
Salmon

(Getting to know—nature's children)
Includes index.
ISBN 0-7172-1917-8

1. Salmon—Juvenile literature.
I. Title. II. Series.

QL638.S2S33 1985 j597'.55 C85-098734-2

Printed and Bound in Canada

Have you ever wondered . . .

Have you ever watched a fish in a fishbowl or aquarium? There is something mysterious about a fish. How can it glide along so silently? How does it breathe under the water? What does it think about all day long?

The salmon is perhaps even more mysterious than most fish. It begins life in fresh water in a river or stream. As a "teenager," it travels downstream to the salty ocean. When the salmon's life is almost over, it fights its way back upstream to the same river or stream where it was born.

Why does the salmon travel so far? What does it do while at sea? How does it find its way back to the river or stream where it was born?

Questions like these have puzzled people for thousands of years. Long ago, storytellers used to say that salmon were really human beings.

These old stories said that the salmon people were princes and princesses. They had beautiful palaces in the depths of the ocean where they lived while they were at sea. When they wanted to come back inland, they put on robes of salmon flesh and swam up the rivers and streams.

Of course, we know today that these stories are not true. However, there is still an air of mystery about the remarkable salmon.

Sleek, slim and beautiful are just a few ways to describe the salmon-- mysterious too!

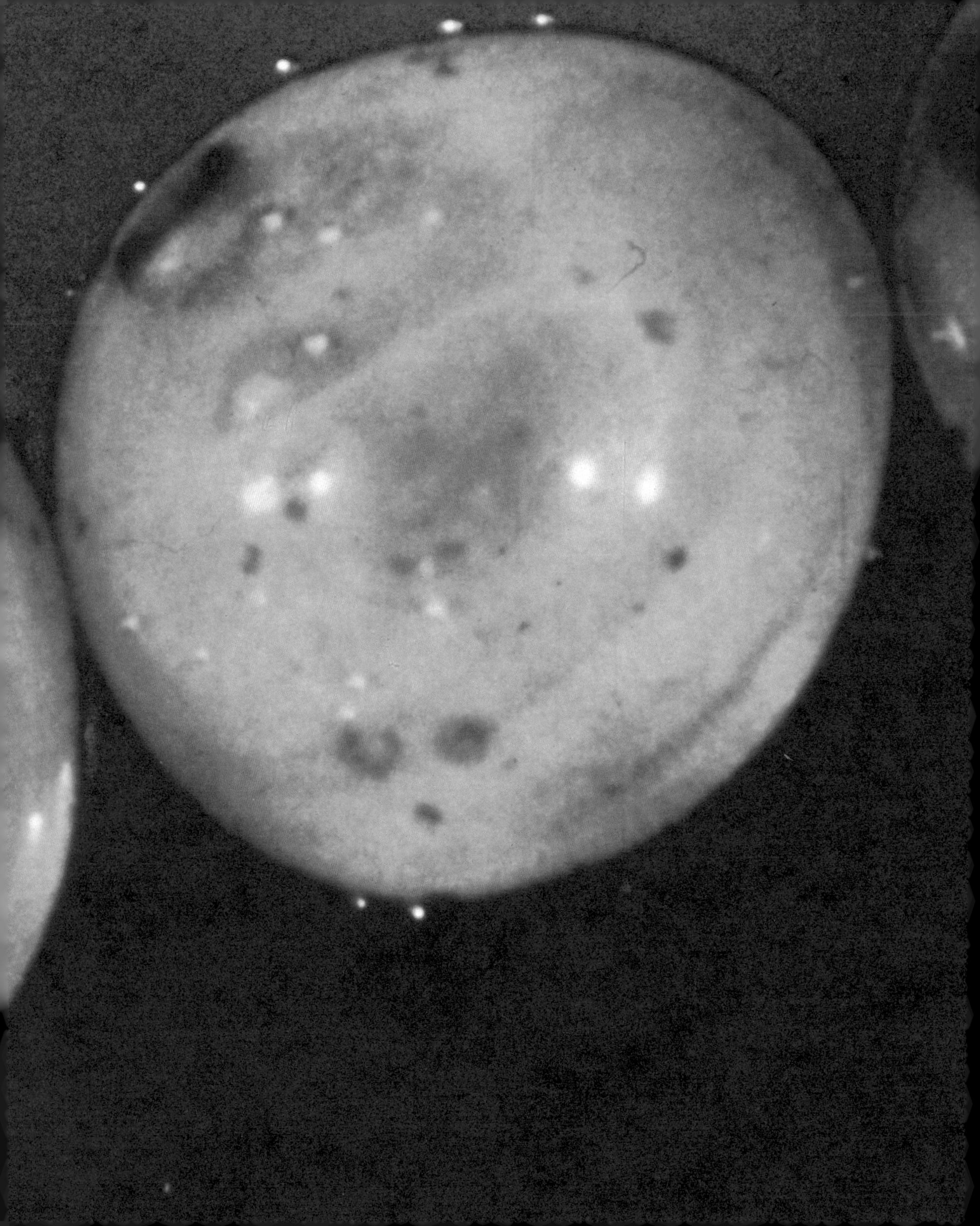

Tiny Pink Eggs

The salmon starts life as a round pink egg no bigger than a pea. The egg lies deep in the gravel under a swift-flowing river or stream. With it are hundreds of other little pink eggs. These will hatch to become the baby salmon's sisters and brothers.

The mother and father salmon will not be there when the eggs hatch. They do not really take care of their young in any way. However, the mother salmon hides her eggs in as safe a place as possible. She covers them with a deep layer of gravel, so that they are out of sight, but still surrounded by flowing water.

A few weeks later, two tiny black specks appear inside each pink egg. These are the eyes of the little creature growing inside.

Salmon eggs magnified to about 40 times their actual size.

Babies with "See-Through" Bodies

Soon the tiny fish begin to struggle inside their rubbery pink shells. This usually happens in late winter or spring. One by one, they break through their shells. Some come out head first, others tail first.

At this stage the baby salmon are called alevins. They have soft, see-through bodies. If you were to look at one, you could see straight through to its ribs and backbone. You would see the tiny heart just behind its mouth, busily pumping red blood.

The little alevin would seem to be staring right back at you. At this stage the baby salmon's eyes are enormous compared with its body.

On the underside of each alevin's body, you would see a round, hanging sac. This is the yolk sac from the alevin's egg. During the first few weeks after hatching, the baby salmon does not eat. Instead, it draws its nourishment from its yolk sac.

Opposite page:

The wide-eyed little alevin never has to worry about where its next meal will come from.

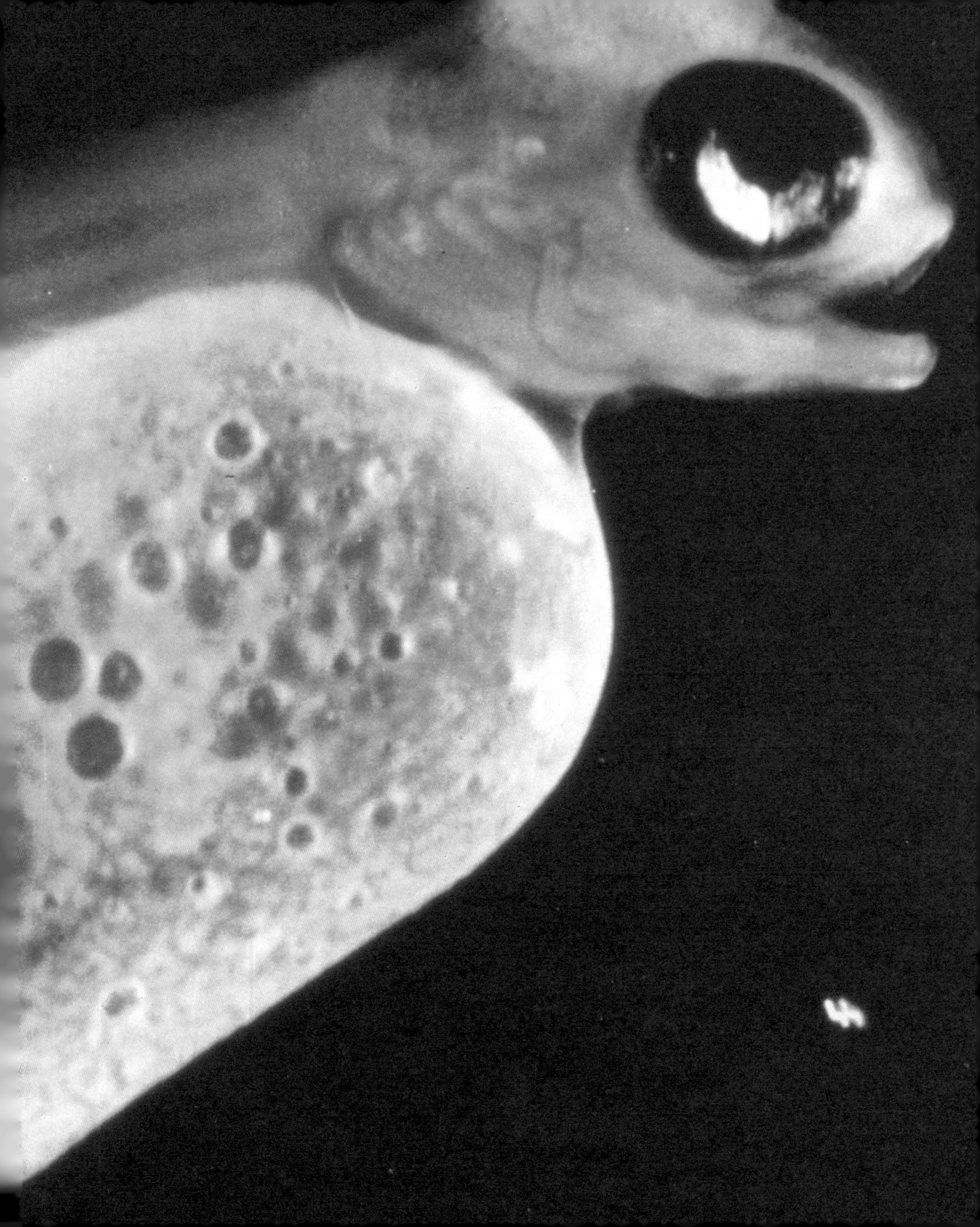

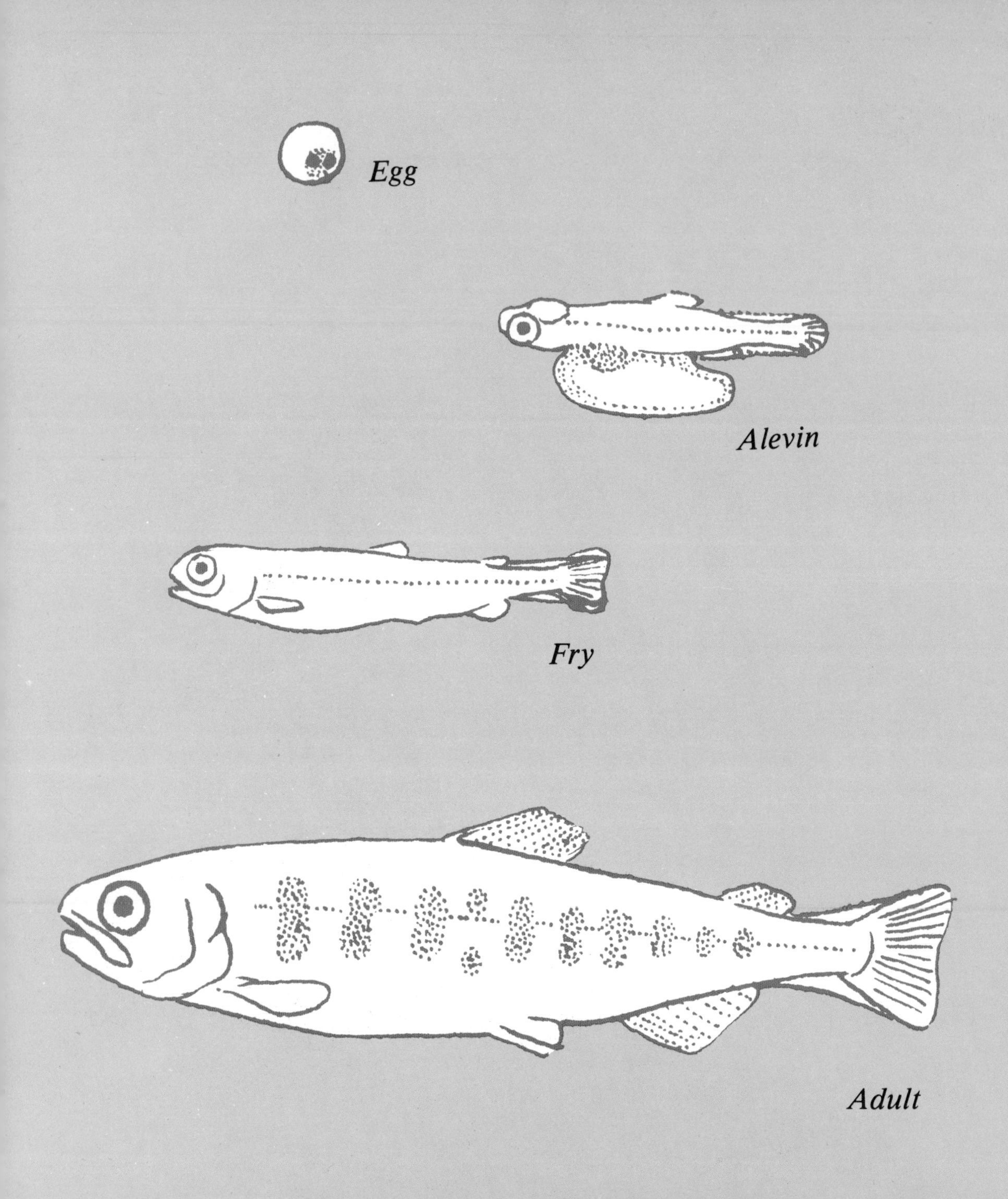
Egg
Alevin
Fry
Adult

Small Fry

After several weeks, the alevins grow restless down in the gravel of their river or stream bed. Little by little they begin to wriggle up toward open water.

As time passes, the alevins' yolk sacs become smaller and smaller. At last the sacs disappear altogether. They have been completely taken up into the bodies of the baby salmon.

Once the baby salmon lose their yolk sacs, they are no longer alevins. They are now known as fry or parr. (Have you ever heard people speak of children as "small fry"? Now you know where this expression comes from!)

Like Real Fish at Last

The salmon fry, although only about two and a half centimetres (one inch) long, look much more like fish now. Tiny scales cover their bodies, and they have small, separate fins.

At first the fry eat any bits of food that happen to drift into their mouths. But soon they learn to go after food themselves. They start off eating the small larvae (hatched eggs) of insects. Gradually, they eat larger larvae and adult insects that fall into the pond. The salmon are strong, quick hunters. They soon learn to leap high out of the water after their prey.

The salmon fry do not only pursue prey. They are also pursued. Trout, perch and many other fish like to gobble up the tasty salmon fry. So do otters, eels and fish-eating birds such as kingfishers.

It's hard to believe that this tiny fish will one day weigh as much as a medium-sized dog.

Down to the Sea

Someday you will become a teenager. During your teen years, many changes will take place in your body. You will change from being a child to being an adult.

The life of the salmon is the same in a way. But the salmon reaches its "teenage" stage at only two to four years of age! Then major changes start taking place in the young fish's body. These changes prepare it to live in the adult world of the salmon—the ocean.

Soon after the changes begin, the young salmon leaves the stream or river where it hatched. It swims downstream toward the ocean along with others of its own kind. Sometimes the journey is as long as 3000 kilometres (1800 miles).

At last the young salmon reach a bay where their stream or river meets the ocean. There they linger for a while, almost as if they are deciding whether to go on or not. Finally, they strike out into the open ocean, where they will spend most of their adult lives.

Fresh Water, Salty Water

If you have ever gone swimming in the ocean, the taste of the water and the slight sting in your eyes may have told you that ocean water is salty.

Unlike ocean water, river and stream water is not salty. We call it fresh water. Some kinds of fish, such as trout, can live only in fresh water.

Some other kinds of fish, such as cod, can live only in salty water. If they swam into fresh water, they would soon die.

The salmon, however, is special. It is one of the few kinds of fish in the world that can live in both fresh and salty water. It is able to do so by increasing or decreasing the amount of salt in its body. The amount of salt changes to balance the amount of salt in the water.

Home, sweet, salmon home.

Cold-water Cousins

There are two main kinds of salmon in the world—Atlantic Salmon and Pacific Salmon. We call them cousins because they all belong to one big family of fish—the *Salmonidae* family.

Both of these salmon live in the northern third of the world. Why? Salmon like to live in cool or cold water. If you went swimming in water at the temperature that salmon like, you would soon start shivering. Salmon like water that is below about 14° C (57° F).

Comparative size of 5 types of Pacific Salmon

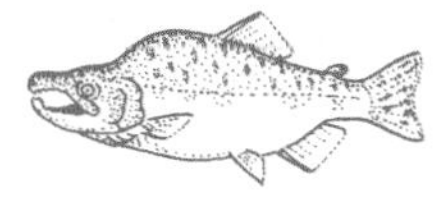

Pink

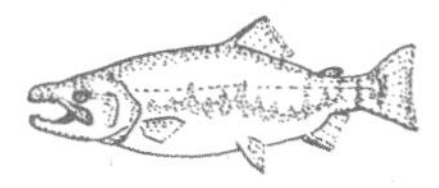

Chum

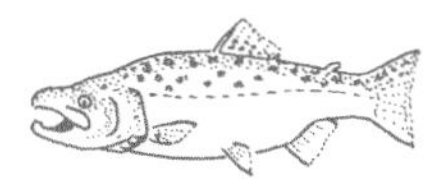

Coho

Sockeye

Chinook

The more the merrier. Salmon, like most fish, often swim in a group called a school.

Atlantic Salmon

Baby Atlantic Salmon hatch in the streams and rivers of Canada's Maritime provinces and Quebec and in those of the northeastern United States. Many Atlantic Salmon also hatch in the streams and rivers of Europe.

When young Atlantic Salmon reach the "teenage" stage, they make their way down to the Atlantic Ocean. Once out in the ocean, many swim far north to Arctic waters.

Pacific Salmon

Pacific Salmon found in North America are divided into five main groups: 1) sockeye 2) chum 3) pink 4) coho 5) chinook. They hatch in the cool streams and swift-flowing rivers of British Columbia and the western United States, down as far as northern California. Some Pacific Salmon are also born in Japan and Siberia.

When young Pacific Salmon reach the "teenage" stage, they make their way down to the Pacific Ocean. Once at sea, many swim far out into the northern Pacific to feed.

Opposite page:

Two salmon passing in the sea.

Collins

Meet the Full-grown Salmon

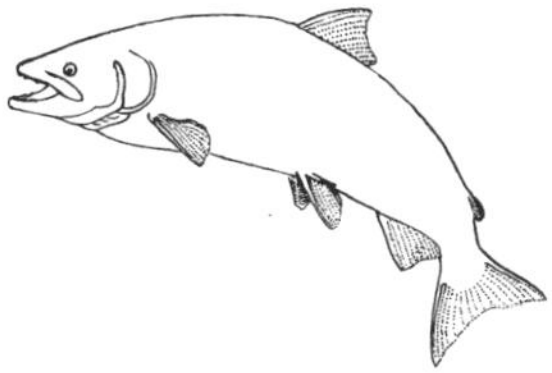

Like many other fish, the salmon has a long streamlined body that helps it glide through the water easily.

Also, like most fish, it is covered with shiny scales that overlap like shingles on a roof. These scales are like a coat of armor. They help protect the fish from injury. Over its scales the salmon has a slimy-feeling coat of mucus. This too protects the salmon by helping it slip over rocks easily so that its scales are not hurt.

Salmon fins

The salmon, like most fish, has several fins to help it swim. Its large V-shaped tail fin acts as a paddle and a rudder. On its belly the salmon has two smaller pairs of fins to help it turn and stop in the water. These small fins also help the salmon hover in the water while feeding. Behind these is a single fin that acts as a keel, holding the salmon upright in the water. The big fin sticking up on the salmon's back acts as a keel too. And the salmon can use the sharp spines on this fin to defend itself from attack by a predator.

Many Sizes, All Cleverly Disguised

Full-grown salmon vary a great deal in size, depending on the kind. Some kinds of salmon are full-grown at one kilogram (2.2 pounds). Others can weigh as much as 55 kilograms (120 pounds). An average full-grown salmon weighs about 13 kilograms (29 pounds) and is about 100 centimetres (40 inches) long. This makes it about as big as a medium-sized dog.

There are many different colors of salmon, but most have dark spots on their sides and backs and silvery colored bellies. There is a very good reason for this two-tone coloring. Seen from above, the salmon's dark spotted back helps it blend in against the rocks and weeds at the bottom. From below the salmon's silvery belly is hard to see against the bright water surface. What a clever disguise to fool predators!

That flash of silver on the salmon's belly not only looks pretty, but it's a useful disguise too.

Breathing Under Water

You breathe because you need oxygen from the air to stay alive. The salmon needs oxygen too. However, it cannot get this oxygen by breathing air as you do. Instead, the salmon gets its oxygen from water.

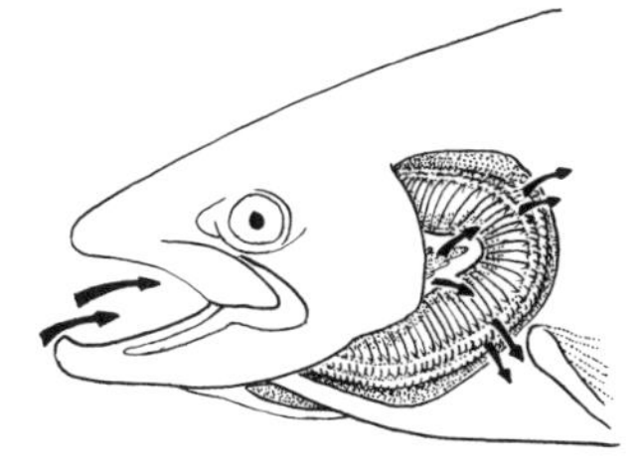

How a salmon breathes through its gills.

To do this, the fish uses its gills. Rounded, flap-like covers protect the gills. You may have noticed the gill covers on a salmon or other fish. They are on the sides of the fish's head, behind the mouth and eyes.

Underneath the gill covers, the salmon's gills are fleshy and bright red. The red color comes from the many small blood vessels in the gills.

As water passes over the salmon's gills, red blood cells in the blood vessels pick up oxygen. The salmon's bloodstream then carries the oxygen through its body. This keeps the fish alive and healthy.

Glubba, glubba, glub glub--Like all fish, a salmon breathes through gills--special slits at the sides of its head.

Let's Eat

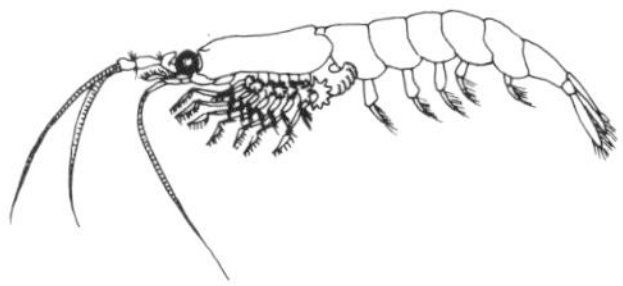

Krill

A pink mass of wriggling creatures covers the ocean surface above a school (group) of salmon. Within the mass, each tiny shining body is rimmed with pink-orange light.

The salmon twist their solid powerful bodies and shoot up toward the surface. Jaws wide open, they hurl themselves at the pink mass, eating as fast as they can. At last all the crisp little pink creatures are gone. Their bellies full, the salmon lazily glide away.

A few hours later, however, the salmon will be hungry again. They will have to look for more food. Perhaps this time they will catch larger, livelier prey such as herring, smelt, small squid or eels. Or if they are lucky, they might come upon another squirming mass of "pink food."

The salmon's "pink food" is made up of shiny shrimplike creatures called krill. During their saltwater years, salmon eat large numbers of krill, as well as true shrimp. It is this diet of pink food that gives the salmon's flesh its pink color.

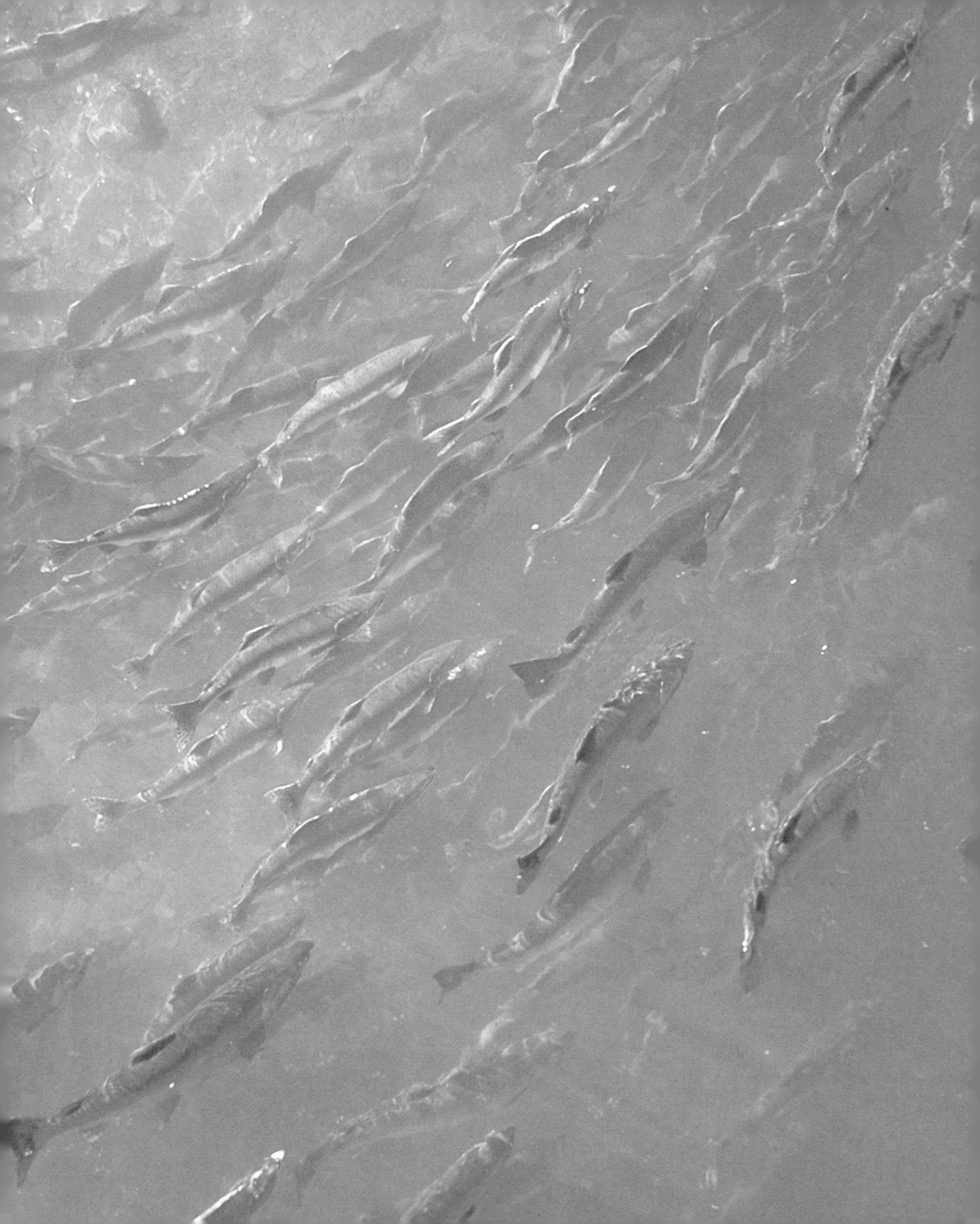

A Dangerous Life

All its life, the salmon must struggle hard to escape predators who would like nothing better than a meal of delicious pink salmon flesh.

Keen-eyed birds such as eagles, Herring Gulls, and cormorants prey upon the ocean-going salmon. Ocean mammals such as seals, Sea Lions, Killer Whales and porpoises also catch and eat salmon. So do sharks and some of the bigger fish, such as cod and tuna. Sometimes, the larger salmon will prey upon smaller salmon.

In many ways, the salmon is still a mystery to people. We really do not know how it thinks or how much it acts on instinct. One thing is certain. Any thinking that the salmon does probably centers on two subjects: how to get enough to eat, and how to avoid being eaten itself!

Finding the Way Home

After two, three or more years at sea, adult salmon leave the ocean and return to fresh water. They head straight for the inland rivers and streams where they were born. How do they know their way?

This question is part of the mystery of the salmon. We do not know the full answer. However, many scientists believe that salmon find their way to the coast by sensing the earth's magnetic field and the ocean's currents. Once they reach the coast their strong sense of smell helps to guide them. Each river has its own special smell, a mixture of all the odors of food, soil, weeds and rocks that are in the water. The salmon detects this smell and follows it home.

It's hard to miss a Pacific Salmon that's returning to spawn. That's because it's body is bright red and its head is grayish-green.

Up from the Sea

Thousands of pink eggs are now growing inside the female salmon's body. The egg mass bulges out on both sides of her body, making her look fat.

The male salmon, on the other hand, becomes thin and fierce looking. His eyes sink far into his head, and his upper jaw hooks down over his lower one. Sperm are ripening in his body. He will use these to fertilize a female's eggs.

From the time the salmon enter fresh water, they stop eating. They do not feel hungry any more. Their bodies live off the fat built up during years of ocean feeding.

Yet the salmon remain strong swimmers. They must be strong to battle their way upstream to their home river or stream. For weeks the salmon struggle against the current. Sometimes churning rapids and waterfalls loom up in their way. The salmon leap high into the air to clear them.

Opposite page:
Not even a waterfall will stop a determined salmon from reaching its spawning ground.

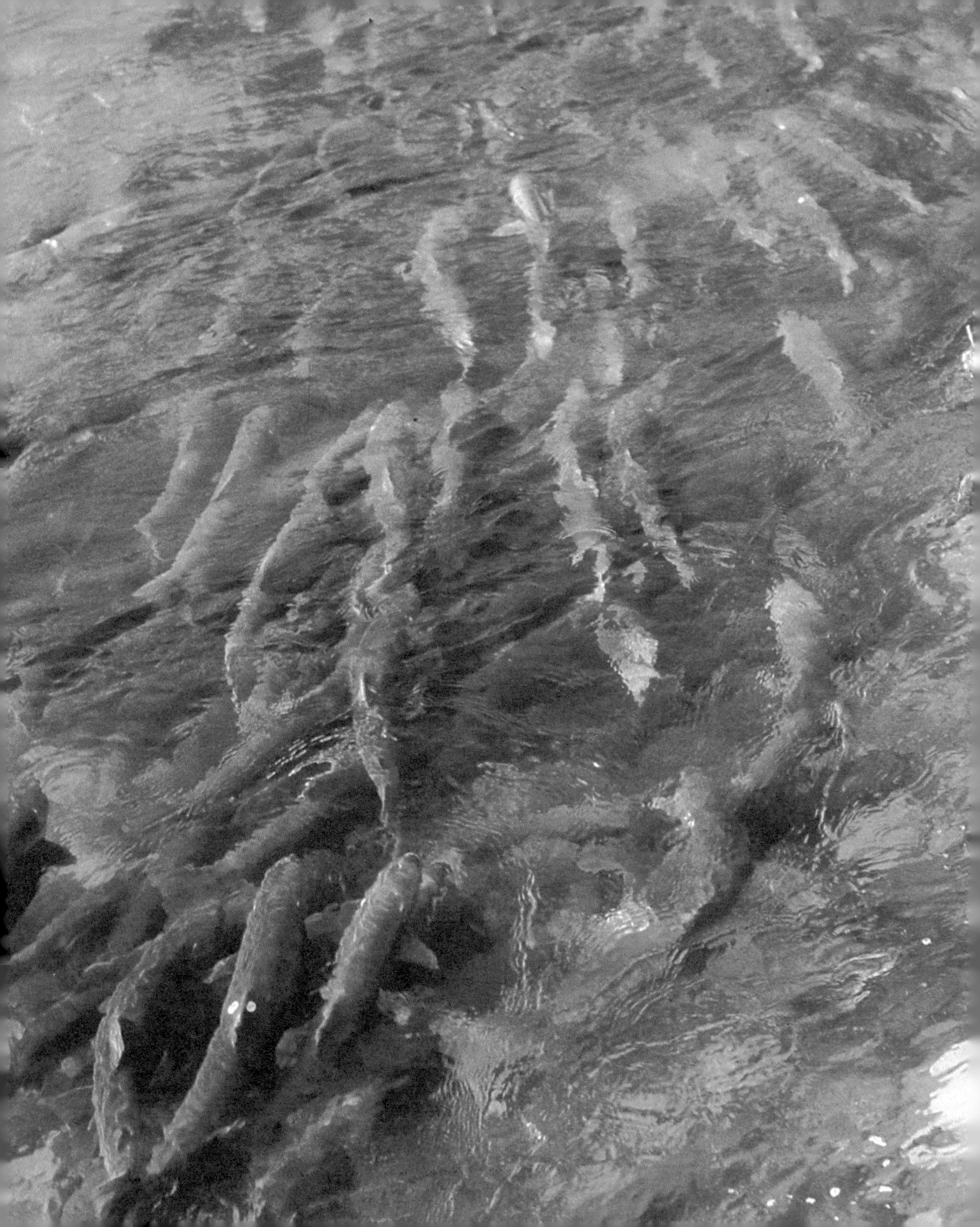

Home at Last

At last the salmon are home. They glide in and out among the same rocks where they swam as "small fry." They rest in the shade of the same trees that leaned out from shore and shaded them when they were young.

The salmon have returned home to spawn. Soon the female salmon begin to search in the gravel at the bottom for good places to dig their nests. Some even fight with each other. The largest and strongest females claim the best nesting areas.

Having chosen her spot, the female rolls over onto her side. She flutters her tail in the gravel of the stream bed, digging a hollow. She rests for a moment and then turns on her side to begin digging again.

Here's a stream that's bursting with life. All these salmon are swimming home to spawn.

New Life

A male salmon swims up beside her. Another follows, also anxious to mate with the female. However, the fierce looking first male charges at the second male and drives him away.

By now the female has used her powerful fluttering tail to make her hollow about half a metre (over a foot and a half) deep. She hovers over it. Hundreds of tiny pale-pink eggs stream from her body.

At that same moment the male salmon, close beside the female, sends out a milky stream of fluid containing his sperm.

The sperm fertilize the eggs, joining with them to start new life growing. It is from the combined eggs and sperm that baby salmon will hatch.

Pacific Salmon moms lay between three and five thousand eggs.

Tired Salmon

What will protect the little eggs till they hatch? The mother salmon takes care of that. She swims upstream and begins to dig a new hollow. Some of the gravel from this new hollow drifts down and covers the fertilized eggs in the first nest.

The mother salmon keeps digging gravel nests and laying her eggs. She may repeat the process up to eight times. Each time the male is right beside her, fertilizing the eggs as she lays them.

At last the female has no more eggs. Both she and the male are tired out. So are the other salmon who have been spawning in the stream.

No longer able to swim against the current, the tired fish begin to drift downstream. They are skinny and sick looking. Their fins are ragged. Their scales are falling off. The withered brown leaves of autumn fall around them. Insects shimmer on the surface of the water. But the weary salmon hardly notice. At last they die.

Opposite page:

Many Atlantic Salmon return to the sea after they spawn.

Life Goes On

Most salmon die after spawning only once. All Pacific Salmon do so. However, some Atlantic Salmon actually live to return to sea. After several years at sea, these "second lifers" come back home to spawn a second time. A few have been known to spawn three or more times.

But this is rare. For most salmon, life is over after one spawning.

This seems sad . . . until we remember the thousands of tiny pink eggs buried in the gravel beneath the rivers and streams. Soon new life inside them will be stirring. Then the story of the salmon will start all over again.

Special Words

Alevin A newly hatched salmon, still with its yolk sac attached.

Blood cells Tiny parts of blood which help to carry oxygen to the rest of the body.

Fins Parts of a fish's body which the fish uses to move itself around or change directions.

Fry A young salmon without its yolk sac. Sometimes also called parr.

Gills Openings in a fish's body that take in oxygen.

Larvae The second stage of an insect's life which occurs after it has hatched from the egg.

Predator An animal that hunts other fish or animals for food.

Prey An animal that is hunted for food.

Spawn To deposit eggs.

Sperm A substance produced by the male to fertilize the eggs.

INDEX

Cover Photo: G. Van Rijckevorsel (Valan Photos)

Photo Credits: G. Van Rijckevorsel (Valan Photos), pages 4, 6, 16, 20, 29, 35, 44; Nova Scotia Department of Fisheries and Oceans, pages 8, 11; Atlantic Salmon Federation, pages 15, 30; Tim Fitzharris (First Light Associated Photographers), page 19; Thomas Kitchin (Valan Photos), page 22; Wilf Schurig (Valan Photos), page 26; H. Armstrong Roberts (Miller Services), pages 33, 39; Dennis W. Schmidt (Valan Photos), pages 36, 40, 43.